Nigeria Beyond Politics

Yusuf Sopeyin

ISBN: 978-1-4834-1003-6 (sc)
ISBN: 978-1-4834-1002-9 (e)

Because of the dynamic nature of the Internet, any web addresses or links contained in this book may have changed since publication and may no longer be valid. The views expressed in this work are solely those of the author and do not necessarily reflect the views of the publisher, and the publisher hereby disclaims any responsibility for them.

Any people depicted in stock imagery provided by Thinkstock are models, and such images are being used for illustrative purposes only. Certain stock imagery © Thinkstock.

Lulu Publishing Services rev. date: 03/26/2014

CONTENTS

ACKNOWLEDGEMENT

I am most indebted to my parents for their love, support, guidance and care always. I could never thank you enough. May Allah reward you beyond your efforts.

Special thanks goes to my wife and

To my siblings whom have all encouraged me.

My teachers and

Also to my family and friends, thank you all.

God bless you.

DEDICATION

In the Name of Allah the most beneficient the most merciful

For Humanity.

PROLOGUE

A people's condition is a state of their mind.

The cliché above explains a people's condition in relation to their mind set. The overtime disposition of people brought about by their subconscious informed psycho mental overview of life and things in general. The precepts that overtime form the collective way of thought of an individual, family, group or society at large. The result of thought formation process brought about by fractions of ideas having formed an ideology with which we observe, analyze, judge and respond to all circumstances at every point in time.

The mind-condition relationship is enormous and cannot be overemphasized. It determines the ideology of a people and their behavioral outcome and condition.

The thrust of this book (Nigeria Dilema) is analyzed from a different dimension (cause), from what used to be the familiar focal point of discussion (problems). Primarily, the condition overtime of Nigeria is untowardly chaotic giving the vast arrays of problems from all dimensions of life that confront us as citizens and those who overtime inhabit her. Problems such as socioeconomic, political, and other human milieu that hold us in a web of despair, bitterness, self pity and anger as well to say a least. The collective dispositionary condition is one of hardships, series upon another and seemingly unending as is evident in the society. We often time identify these problems and extensively espouse on the negative consequences that we have had to face as a people, however, without identifying the cause which is actually the main issue and the most important reference point at rectifying the problems from the bottom in order to uproot the problems from their root cause so as to eliminate them once and for all. The human habit perhaps is a huge challenge, it is thus very important to first put this into consideration in order to understand where we are coming from so as to have a clear vision of the issue we are dealing with as well as understanding where we hope to head. In order to arrive at a desired destination.

The dispositionary attitude of the people hasn't been too forward looking in terms of growth and development. One informed by a "Psycho mental Distortion". The first step at solving any problem is the identification of the cause or the source of the problem. Without that the problem cannot be solved. The good news is that the problem is not one without a cure but, that once realized and dealt with rightly, we are about to turn a new chapter, rewrite history and change our condition once we retune our minds to positive and forward looking thoughts, tolerant, productive, loving, accommodating and peaceful outlook and united above all in a common pursuit towards a desirable condition for all of us.

No single person is particularly better than another other than their mind and attitudinal disposition towards life and people in general. Respect for humanity, love, peace, tolerance and acceptance are all key to humanity and a forward looking society. One that breeds progress, comfort and security for all members of such a society.

Problems are first internal than external. The cause of a problem is first within and no matter how much of an external approach sought, if the root cause is not firstly discovered or ascertained the problem will forever persist. Hypothetically an ailment or a sickness is first diagnosed by the medical doctor before treatment is administered and this procedure is very important as is fundamental in the medical practice. The doctors are trained to carry out as a first procedure a diagnosis of the problem before treatment is considered. It is very applicable in every aspect of human life. Regarding our every day issues, we must first of all find out the cause of our problems before any meaningful solution is sought else the problem would persist for as long as the real cause of the problem is not ascertained. Remember, the most important step to solving any problem is finding the cause of the problem. It is easily the hardest thing to do in most cases, partly because it is half the problem solved. "in life we do not need a solid ground but the dexterity of a swimmer". Depending on how you look at it, life primarily was designed with everything in abundance, most times however we always demand for a perfect scenario, where as that perfect scenario is ours to shape. It is like having all the tools you need to shape something, anything, however if you do not make attempt at it you don't even get started not to talk of advancing further. That is the reality of life scenario, life doesn't present everything we need to us one hundred percent perfectly as we want it readily, it always shows up in a disguised form and manner in such a way that it wants us to identify it, take it as well as shape it into the best and most suitable form for us. The reaction of human beings generally to this unique nature of life is what defines them in totality of their daily existence as it involves all aspects of their human endeavors.

For example, individuals, groups and society always blame government for their problem generally, however government may be involved, the truth is at the level of that problem whether individual, group or societal, the problem must be approached from the level of the problem. For example an individual who has no education blames the government, or his parents, where as another individual with a similar problem sees the end result therefore seeks a personal solution to their problem knowing well that is the fastest solution rather than blaming people or lamenting all their lives and accusing a government that is deaf to such plights. Such attitudes only result into bitter counter effects and worse more an ideological trap. It should be made clear that the fundamental structure of society is the commonness of its people and this doesn't mean that a society must be monolithic in its ideology, rather convergent upon its goals in its multicultural outlook. Meaning that we must as is often said be able to "agree to disagree". It does not mean that we have to adopt ideologies that are against our beliefs rather, that we must tolerate it in as much as they form the values of others and do not clash with humanity. societal pluralism thus implies that people must have varied ideological leanings and beliefs and no matter how divergent they are we must all find a common ground at reaching the larger and common goal of the society which is just and equal rights and opportunities for all members of the society.

Therefore in the case of Nigeria, our problem is not in our multiplicity as a diverse and multiethnic nation, rather, it lies in our greed, the inability of the divides to find a common ground, a common purpose and a common voice to push away all ideological and often sentimental divides thus embracing a collective approach and sincerely adopting a genuine collective interest for the whole citizens of the nation as the solution to our long held problems.

The solution to our problems are no more than our rising up collectively against the threshold of our limiting mindsets, thus lifting the barrier over our reasoning.

It is time to really look inwards and realize our position In order to push forward a common goal of equal opportunities, respect, justice and equity in the society. ones built upon trust, hope and dedication to the country.

I hope that my courage of the conviction of a better future for the Nation, driven by a mind reformed people, positive and forward looking, one which inspired me in writing this book would likewise inspire everyone to believe and work towards the common good of our dear Country and humanity at large.

God bless you.

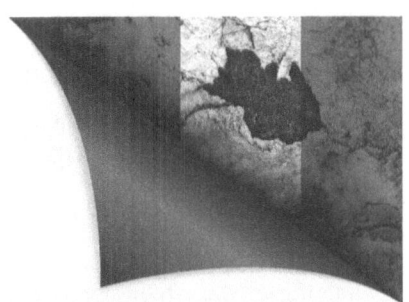

CHAPTER ONE

VALUES, TRADITIONS, CULTURES AND IDEOLOGY

According to various scholars, definitions to the above terms abound. Here however, we examine specific definitions for our purpose.

Value, according to Gordon Alport is "a belief upon which a man acts by preference". The concise form of this definition makes it easily adoptable for our discussion, on the other hand, Tradition can be defined according to the Chambers dictionary as "the process of passing on from one generation to generation, customs, beliefs, stories e.t.c while culture by the Encyclopedia Britannica is defined as "the way of life and the characteristic artifact produced by a group of people over a period of time". The essence of the definitions is to nexus the three terms and bring them to bear on the larger concept, Ideology. It is important now to ask a fundamental Question. "how have our values, traditions and cultures shaped our condition as a people?

The multicultural outlook of Nigeria as a nation state makes the understanding of the dimensions through which these concepts(values, traditions, cultures and ideologies) affect the country. The problem of Nigeria giving the dimensions of ideological differences is complex and complex at once. The complexity is such that the interplay of ideological differences has led to a constant clash of general considerations in terms of socio-economic development leading to stagnations and decay of existing structures.

Historically, the condition of Nigeria in pre-colonial era was one of a people with no formal education. Majorly agrarian with no mechanized means of farming and its cultivation. The system of government was one of kingdoms and kings-subjects relationships where the kings were overlords. The housing structures and dwellings were characterized by mud and thatches, people engaged in all sorts of trades such as artifacts, crafts, clothing's, farm produce and jewelries. There were occasional inter communal clashes between kingdoms which often led to seizures of people into slavery. It was a struggle of the strong against the weak. The nation state called Nigeria today was not really defined before the influx of the western invaders who either came for all kinds of trade purposes such as slave trade. The major tribes remain the Hausa, Igbo and the Yoruba as well as other less populated tribes such as the Edo, Fulani, Kanuri, Ijaw, Tiv, Calabari and a lot more. After the surge of the Europeans and the particular colonial occupation of the British, There was an amalgamation which fused all these tribes into one entity however territorially distinguishing the lot into North, South, West and East. The Name Nigeria was conceived obviously owing its influence to the river Niger which cuts into the geographical landscape of the country through the North-west, North-East and adjoining at the Centre to cut through to the south. Then the fate of the nation was defined, a country of multi ethnic fronts about to embark on a journey of National conformation in what would later be defined by bloody coups and counter coups, post colonialisation, which were defined by ethnic and tribal motivations, a result of an unenvisaged and hasty Nationalization of a people unready for such pact. The eventual consequence being the pursuit of regional interests, ones which actually are blighted by groups or individual interests, thus defeating the disguised motive. Most politicians' motive of looking after their regional interests is often counter effective resulting in a rather selfish and personal interests often. This has been the order of the polity over time since independence and there seems still not to be a defined purpose for governance since politicians and government have often been unyielding to the needs of those whose interests they pretend to protect. The political terrain and polity which actually defines governance and policies are built on wicked, selfish and inhuman principles in most cases. Instead of looking out for the collective emergence and the welfare of the Nation as a whole, it is rather a divided interest pursuit which eventually results in a counterproductive scenario. It must be asserted that until a national interest policy is first put in place as well as regional and unproductive interest is pushed aside, there would never be a positive change in the nation, instead, it will continue to be the same old story and situation that existed, a sorry state where corruption and injustice thrives with arrant disregard for the rule of law and the conformation of those people who form the country and their constitution of those laws.

The problem of ideology is strongly tied to values, traditional and cultural clinging which obviously have limiting effects on objective reasoning. When much of our value judgment are tied to remote, myopic and specific ideological clinging in a multiple society, it blurs the vision for prosperity and often leads to undesirable conditions as has been in Nigeria overtime, however we must thus learn to live with other people based on their ideology as well in as much as they do not clash nor cross the boundary of humanity. The manner and way by which the values, traditions and cultural ideology have affected the country cannot be overemphasized because they have been reflected overtime in the outcome of our dispositionary condition as a people. One of such observation is the socio-political situation of the nation. The polity is one of such that the political class have often time been constituted by mediocre, charlatans and individuals who first of all have no business in politics because they lack the qualifications to represent the people. With regards to the fact that the ruled are not opposed to such irregularity though in a peaceful and persistent demand for what must be entrenched in law and order is an obvious proof of the ideological values of the vast majority of the populace as a people.

The social structure is one of irregularities, in the sense that there is little or no organization where it matters, as most times things are done arbitrarily without a concrete plan and backup in case of the reoccurrence of such inconsistencies in the future. One of languidity, a languidity of a people on the purpose of humanity. It is important that we observe the socio-cultural antecedent of the Nation, Nigeria once again in relation to an obvious lapse, a desire for improvement in human condition or a search for healthy inquiries into making human lively condition better. Pre-colonial Nigeria was very much uncivilized as we observed, that the earlier slave traders enslaved our people with mere mirrors and other flimsy gifts such as walking sticks, more so haven arrived in ships of sizes that have never been heard of or seen by these people in those ages speak of the level of remoteness and lack of advancement that had preceded us as a people. As at that time the slave traders and their cohort African elite, made up of the kings, chiefs and the rich class amongst those who engaged in making the forceful abdication, torture and execution of the slaves were rudderless and wicked. It isn't time to nurture anger or bitterness, rather the need of an antecedent proof necessary to remind ourselves of the faulty past so as to cleanse our minds of the debris of such attitudes which led to division, obtrusion and a psycho mental Distortion. To look back at our antecedent precondition and realize how we had always reasoned and why it affects us till date, one which we have always failed to see nor realize and none the less think of correcting in order to look forward towards a positive lasting and effective change.

Giving the historical antecedent, not much seems to have changed, as what characterized our dispositionary outlook still shapes our reasoning in terms of our overall and collective ideological state of mind. Though slave trade long ended as well as colonial occupation we still cling on the effects of slavery and colonialism as the cause of our present dilemma, Even when we are the ones governing ourselves and are responsible for the policies that we proffer for our country and nation. Perhaps what remains now is Mental Slavery. A condition one easily observes in the academics even with all the academic or educational qualifications people claim to have attained in the Schools, they remain naïve and illogical to realistic perspectives. Mostly parochial and lacking objectivity in analogical sense of reasoning thus remaining enslaved in academic bigotry. A non african once described Africans saying, "you people are smart, but your problem is, you don't use your sense". Objectively and truly it is very correct and non racial the least. Until we look inward and realize how we are responsible for the injustice, the oppression and maltreatment we suffer in general as a people will we realize that it is then that we have started the real first step at solving the enormous problems that confront us and that in fact it is half of the problem solved. An example from earlier times is how it was our people that first of all were allies and cohorts to the slave traders making way for them to penetrate and easily take the people away as slaves. Our own people sold our men away into slavery and ironically same exist this day although in a worse and more depressing form (Intellectual slavery). For example, Economic policies wrongly adopted by our leaders for selfish ends at the expense of the masses. Most of the crimes committed on us are aided by our leaders who sell us away. Ones of greed, selfishness, hatred for one another and much of arrogance and intolerance all of which is based on an abyss of ignorance. The limiting effect of the overtime held ideological predisposition brought about by our values, traditions, and cultures overtime has been unrealized as the real cause of our overtime dilemma. The problem of mindset still. "Education is not learning but life". Where education helps us to be free of naivety, it is supposed to lift the lid of obtrusion and lack of objectivity from our reasoning thus giving us a clear and proper perspective to every issue and where we lack knowledge we seek such before making our judgment, less we become faulty and appear like educated fools and ignoramuses (a lot of people still, fall into this category) who commit gross error of judgment because they often view issues through the prism of their closed mindedness and ideological bigotry, they lack the required information or knowledge of the real situation with which to analyze.

True values are humanistic and progressive above all however diverse they are. It is important we review our ideology based values, traditions and cultural outlook in order to push forward and beyond our long held closed mindedness and intolerance as it cuts across all human areas of life.

An inquiry into the mindset of a typical African condition has proven unique in the sense that when you look around the entire sub-Saharan African continent the same problems confront us. Don't get me wrong, what I am about to reveal is the beginning of a beautiful change, a positive change and an effective eye opener, for when the philosopher is naïve too then he seizes to be a philosopher in its truest sense. The Psycho mental Distortion earlier mentioned is a huge dilemma, one that confronts the African mind. The attitude is very fundamental to this problem as it has to do topically with this chapter with all its terms spelt out. First of all it has been observed in my careful inquiry of the root cause of our problems, that the most fundamental starting with, is our values, cultures and traditions. The general sum up which builds up into our ideological seal up. Our dispositionary rigidity and inability to think for ourselves holistically and independently with the confidence required to assert what we consider a truism or at least a hypothesis. For example, of all the academic works and standards set across the world, what is the most tangible contribution of Africa and by Africa I don't mean Africans who have thrived in western worlds as a result of their western exposure, rather I mean a real, concrete and concerted effort of Africa by Africans to advance knowledge beyond where it is at any of its levels anywhere in the world. Rather what you find all over is wars, division, underdevelopment, leaders clinching their fist on power and refusing to let go of it as well as a high level of corruption and crimes amongst many problems visible. A unique experience across Africa. An objective reasoning is one which leads one to an even critical examination of oneself as a diagnosis of one's errors or problems before looking outside of oneself. Majority of times we bitterly blame the west for our problems and sadly it is a huge trap. A very big error of judgment that results from a huge emotional weakness, one that often results into a lack of hindsight, however the need for a sensible approach, one which is critical and forward looking as well as liberating from the gouge of mental emotionalism. As a people we must realize that to absolve oneself of fault and lay blames on others is to resolve that we are not in control of our own lives or destiny, that rather those whom we blame and hold responsible are in charge of our own lives and that they are the ones who are responsible for our own lives and circumstances. It is self defeating and a very dangerous belief and outlook as well. This is the true picture of our reality, one which we have always failed to realize and change. A typical disposition of ours concerning the approach of always trying to calm the ailment rather than curing it. Example is adopting foreign policies that are not practical with the reality on ground, no matter how much we try to posit policies in the face of a dilemma whose root cause has not yet been identified we cannot get beyond that dilemma no matter how successful such policies have been elsewhere because they are unique to the problems of their original source or locations where they were conceived and there were antecedent rationalization that brought about such policies and unique to the root cause of their problems. Logically importing policies and thinking they would solve our problems without looking through the unique situation of our own problems is being naïve as well as lacking the common sense to chart our own cause of enlightenment and independence in terms of achieving a meaningful development and stability required to arrive at prosperity for the generality of our people. Intellectual Naivety is a gross problem, not implying that everyone suffers from it, thought asserting that the unique cause of the problem of our nation is this and if we do not realign our attitudes to that of positivity, confidence, resourcefulness and pro activeness, we will for long wallow in a trap of dependence upon those and the rest of the world who have gone beyond naivety and have overcome naivety in all its facets and achieve success for themselves.

The dangers of rigid mind traps is huge and impending especially when it has not been realized. It is very important to correct any of our limiting values, traditions and cultural outlook to positive, objective and forward looking ones in all of our affairs especially national ones as it affects every member of the society.

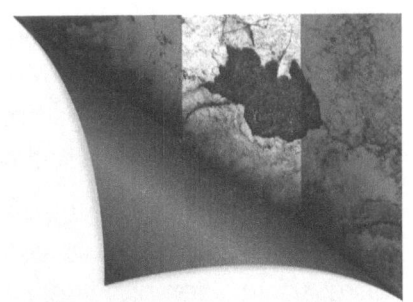

CHAPTER TWO

POLITICS, LEADERSHIP AND GOVERNANCE

The issue of politics, leadership and governance has long been in existence since the beginning of time, more so as men multiplied, families evolved and societies became complex with increasing numbers of people involved, the need for leadership, political gathering, association and governance became important as the complexity of human societies meant that it was necessary for such or else there would exist a society where men chose to behave in any manner that pleases them. The fear of anarchy and chaos led to the formation of authorities and governance through which the society comforts and is assured peace. The collective good therefore is the principle with which governance is established irrespective of ideologies giving that the common good holds sway in all manner to protect humanity or the general good. However, since the earliest known beginnings where politics, governance and leadership arose there has been problems upon another, problems of dissatisfaction amongst others which confront the entire human societies. The problems of whether the individuals entrusted with leadership will do justly and deliver the expectations of the task they are entrusted. Whether they will serve the society whose interest is the reason they are in office the first place. Often times the people who form the core of the society are often underserved by their leaders whereby it often results in discontent, protests, uprisings, riots, coups or wars. But realistically governance more so leadership are not easy tasks, this is because human beings are very difficult to satisfy, no matter what measures you take or what policies you enact there must be caution at ensuring that such policies are neutral at meeting the common good of the society and that they do not pose a threat to humanity. the structure of governance therefore must be humanistic in the sense that there must be a fair system for all within the society. The establishment of structures that protect the weakest individual in the society and not without as well being just to all and sundry. But in real case scenario this hardly exist as there is either impunity, abuse of power and disregard for the rule of law which holds all bound by the ideal principles that secures such societies thus posing a great threat to the peace of all and humanity as is the essence of such positions. To safeguard every member of the society through existing laws, policies and service institutions at ensuring that good governance is ably administered.

In the case of Nigeria, gauging the position of the country from an historical antecedent of her overtime societal condition. That the complexity of multiplicity of the people that constitute the Nation made the problem as a matter of fact more complex. Giving the differences in ideological divides of all forms some of which are values, tribe, culture, gender, regional, politics and religion amongst others. However the basis or need for any leadership is primarily a result of the association of people who form a society or whom collectively cohabit within the framework of a common geographical position or boundary. Whereas the situation of the country and continent so far has predominantly been that of injustice, social unfairness, huge economic gaps, impunity, intransparency and lawlessness by government administrations that overtime control the affairs of the nation. The character of the individuals who are responsible for governance must first be questioned in relation to the cause, the reason why they could not effect a change or why they further worsened the situation giving the period of time of their leadership and governance. Also the political association they belonged, and the policies and ideology of such parties as regards why the resultant effect of their representative failed are all areas we shall examine as well as why the electorate who hold the electoral powers have contributed to the failure of governance within their responsibilities as electorates.

To start with, when we trace the political/government structure of the Nation since independence we would realize that there have been irregularities as regards the kind of divisional politics that was played, it was more of selfish concerns for regional favoritism from the top. Most times a lot of people emphasize grassroots but you realize the system of governance is very unproductive because it doesn't support the grass roots where the real involvement of all and sundry where real developmental efforts can be achieved. For example the local government councils which are actually closer to the people than the state and federal governments. The structure of governance itself is quite rigid and not designed to be productive to the full extent of governance and service to the people. The federal system structure whereby the states are incapable of carrying out Major possible development actions on their own without the approval of the federal government. The bureaucratic nature of growth and development hindrances brought about by negative agenda backed policies and governance structures have obviously left our nation in an abyss of milieu in all spheres of human lives. Corruption, poverty, unemployment, poor health conditions, underdevelopment amongst several other problems that confront us. The most potent proof is the poverty level of the Nation, yet in abundance of vast natural resources amongst which crude oil is foremost. The government have squandered and worsened from bad scenarios since 1960 into worsening conditions till date. Perhaps we must look back in time and assert the true scenario of our nation before independence, when our colonial masters were in charge, the socio-economic condition of our nation was far better than any government situation headed by our own people since independence. Evidences abound one of which is the exchange rate of the Nation in comparison between the two periods. Another one is the per capita Income of the average Nigerian as at pre independence compared to the best case scenario since independence to date. Also we could use the poverty gap comparison between these periods. From our objective analogical reasoning and conclusion it is very easily conclude-able that governance worsened when we became independent of our colonial masters. This brings us to another reality, a reality we probably never understood. While we criticized colonialism, the question we should be asking is, did it really do us more good or harm? This is the big question we need to ask ourselves, importantly more so, it will help us arrive at the objective basis with which we will arrive at a honest conclusion and answer at realizing the real cause of our problems as it affects this chapter, topically.

Obviously, social and economic conditions worsened as a result of independence. Early into our independence, our Nation witnessed its first bloody coup, a coup which was tribally motivated which also led to a counter coup. All this still holds a place in history and still flashes in the memory of those who perhaps suffered its blow as well as those who remain sympathetic to what they deem a tribal or regional solidarity. The polity, thus has been firstly one of regional solidarity, one which contributes largely to the political problems of our nation. Except we review this problem we will never get beyond its resultant negative implications. Over the years we have pretended as if this is not a problem, however it is such a big hindrance to National advancement. While there is no problem in people representing their regions, but where it affects the collective good whereby some regions are threatened by exclusion through rotational leadership then it is bad and counterproductive for national development. As far as the beginning of humanity, men have always felt threatened by the fear of exclusion thus the struggle to protect self interest, however if effective and right structures are effected then people irrespective of who carriers the leadership banner are less concerned because they feel a sense of true justice as well as protection against exclusion. But I strongly think that the fear of self favoritism is first of all a motivation of selfishness, one brought about by a hidden motive, the motive which could be to first look after oneself instead of a collective good. As well as the need to always be in charge so as to maintain a constant look over self, tribe or region at the expense of a collective good. All this can also be viewed from the point of negative agenda. It is very untoward and ineffective if we continue in the way we are headed because the resultant effect could be worse than before. Like an onlooker and a concerned citizen as well, I do not claim by this book to know all the solutions at once, rather I believe I might have found the right prism to identify the real causes of our problems however they appear, of any form. I believe in the dogma that posits "in life we do not need a solid ground but the dexterity of a swimmer". I hope through this book to awaken our intellectual naivety, to engage us all including myself to think together for once, peacefully objectively and progressively in order to find a real solution to our problems.

The present situation is one of observation as all quarters or regions are watching with care and caution. Giving the fast pace by which societies are evolving and awareness is spreading, it is obvious that the scenario is more dangerous than before and that a real solution is really needed one which is inward and sincere at nipping the problems in the bud once and at least for all. Pragmatically, we can observe that every struggle creates a further struggle and in perspective people who take advantage of such struggles for personal agenda which are the cause of further explosion of the already bad condition. It is important to reorganize the political ideology generally, one which is inclusive, honest and beneficial to all and sundry in order to have a lasting solution and peace at least within the system. Maybe it is time to truly look beyond our naïve mindset and form for the first time a collective National alliance, one that proposes stability in all spheres of life and proposes a forward looking model in all the ramifications of human endeavor. A collective and common voice one which is based upon a sincere collective interest. An agenda which must be against tribalism rather pro national because that is the only true solution to the problem of tribal politics. A polity that is free of selfishness and inconsiderate demands and positions across boards. A sense of justice is what is required and a constant objective reflective prism with which to maintain justice and equity as well as development.

Leadership should not and must not be forced as a principle, this is because leadership requires a huge responsibility and such responsibilities must be upheld in such positions no matter how difficult they are, this is because the expectancy of leadership is huge. Often times leaders in Nigeria and Africa persist in office, some do everything possible to remain in office and refuse to leave after their due date. They arrantly disregard the logic that brought them there. The effect of this is a lack of respect for nationalism, the association of the vast population of citizens that make up the nation. The leadership idea in our Nation is that of rulership, whereas it is supposed to be that of servantship. A leader must be a servant in the truest sense and not an autocrat who sees the citizens as his slaves whom he can malign, leadership is thus a privilege given to only a few in trust of the whole nation, therefore leaders must be astute to their position and sincere to the oath they take with its complete implication. And maybe as a new political paradigm, leaders as a first effective step must legally be enforced to absolve themselves of partisanship once emerged leaders and be made to uphold nationalism in favor of all citizens and members of the society at large. Hoping that in that way there would be a sense of sincere service and productivity whereby they are not too indebted to partisanship but rather to true national cause.

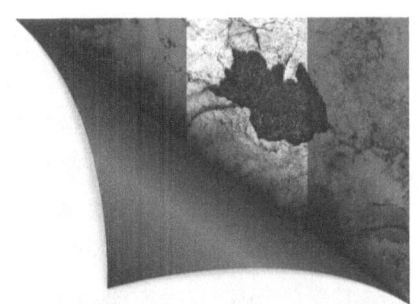

CHAPTER THREE

ECONOMY

I have leveraged the advantage of my knowledge of economics as well as the knowledge of philosophical reasoning to help bring to bear this chapter on the real cause as well of the economic problems that we have suffered over the years. I realized that the solution to the economic problems of any country though policy inclined is not lack of policies but, actually the lack of realistic, effective and direct solution inclined positive policies at meeting the real demands of the complex nature of the entangled economic problems that confront such a Nation. The inability to understand the peculiarity of economic situation and the agents that make up the economic behaviour of such community in order to proffer economic tailored policies, effective to its uniqueness. Since we have based the essence of this book on the cause rather than the problems in themselves in order to achieve a clear objective as to prescribing the right policies aimed at achieving a real and long term sustained positive driven economic growth and development for the nation. In this chapter we will see the effect of concepts on economics and the result of naivety is brought to bear. Thus, to proceed, we must probe into the driving questions as are essential to this chapter, what is the real cause of the economic dilemma that Nigeria as a nation has since plunged into at independence? Why is it that the nation was better off during colonial era economically than the best economic period ever attained since independence? Or alas, should this be a wrong question or assertion? Hopefully we have a concrete framework to juxtapose both era vis a vis economic prosperity as regards real growth and overall positive impact on human welfare in general.? What is the aim of economics itself? What is the economic pursuit or foresight of any reasonable government or economy? What is our main economic outlook? Are we being fooled to look too much outward rather than look at the basis for which any economy is found {could it be economic prosperity of all its citizens?}, is this the underlying characteristics of the economic policies of leading economies the world over? International alliances have been formed by nations who have today grown beyond our common knowledge of the reason for which they came to being, the primary essence which is to protect their overall economic interest above all. It is commonsensical then to think that any alliance with such institutions or organizations by any third parties would derail the basis for which such associations come to being? It is now that my mission of these questions would be unravelled to the reader in case you haven't realized it yet. Of all these thoughts giving the economic complexity of the world today as well as globalization, is it rational to assert that the objective of every economic agent is to prosper, however at the expense of others! Is this the real behaviour of "Positive Economics"? This could lead us to more assertive questions like, how do economic agents behave? Is economics itself based on competition? What is the overall effect of competitive advantage in economics? Is competitive advantage the loss of some and the gain of others? What then is the outlook of Nigeria as an economic agent, her national economic strategy and policies, what aim are they established upon? Then the question of how do we achieve our objectives in a multiple, complex and competitive globalized world without compromising our objectives? Does Nigeria have a strategy at all? These are the objective prisms through which I propose this chapter by aim of first looking inward and identifying the foundation upon which our economics is built. The reality is that our economic policies overtime must have been built on wrong values where as no matter what policy measures taken there cannot be any real positive solution to the economy, this is because such policies would have only been wrongly applied just like it could be likened to administering a wrong medication for an ailment. Though it seems an action is being taken however it is a wrong one because no matter how timely it is administered it would not solve the problem because it is a wrong medication. Unless the exact and applicable medication is administered could there be an improvement in the health condition of such a patient, otherwise the effort of a wrong medication no matter how expensive it is would eventually be costly and unproductive for obvious reasons. Therefore like in economy and its economics, we must ask a fundamental question as it regards the overall good of our economy, have our governments applied the right policies on our economic affairs so far? Is the principle upon which our economic mission is built sound? If so, why then do we still not get it right? what then is the economic problem of our ailing nation? Is it social? Perhaps Political? So many questions! However complex an extent as we have driven this chapter we must realize that it is the right step in the best direction because eventually whether we like it or not there is a question of what is the real cause of the problem and there is an answer, and it is exactly the most important task or endeavour at providing the solution to our economic challenges.

The lay men know what economic problems confront them day by day and much as it is part of economics to identify these problems, the most important task however is the ability to point out the causes and the provision of real time solutions to these problems. Although said, we cannot for the purpose of significance and direction not talk about some fundamental problems here from the perspective of economics in order to grasp fully the extent of economic decay that has overtime affected our nation Nigeria.

Energy supply and electricity is a huge necessity and phenomenon, one which is very essential in modern day economic growth drive. Any nation that lacks electricity is disadvantaged economically and that is a known fact. The extent to which energy is fundamental to economic and national development in this modern day cannot be overemphasized, in fact much of technology and its advancement revolves around energy. Especially electricity, which is sanguine to power generation in industries, firms, hospitals, homes and every other area of economy. To have a non functional electrical power generation nationally is one of the biggest economic problems any nation state must be facing. Nigeria no doubt we all know till present times has yet to solve the problems of electric power instability, shortage, malfunctioning, lack of control, amongst all the problems that confronts it. It is unfortunate to say in the least manner how bad it is that rather than fix electric power the government has opened our doors to all sorts of generating plants, these plants unfortunately add up to the GDP of those nations producing them as well as further depleting our revenue and worse more create environmental pollution and huge noise all over the cities. The health implication of the smoke produced by these generating plants is adverse to human well being as well as having an implication on healthcare.

The effect of over reliance on petroleum is a very chaotic situation because while the nation generates a lot of national income from the sale of crude oil it is very bad that much of the crude oil resources have not been utilized to its full extent. We are only exploring at the primary level, whereby after which we export same for refining purposes. This is the most non-smart economics one can think of especially in a nation where a huge human capital as well as natural resources exist. The lack of perspective and proper understanding of real economic framework by policy makers is one of the contributing problems we have. When government starts to realize that the issue of economy is very huge and must be given the huge attention it deserves like every other serious nations would we start to proffer real time solutions to the economic problems that surmount the nation overtime. It is indeed very important to emphasize that there is a huge economic prospect and way beyond whatever wealth we are realizing now in terms of our national income. If we put our economy in proper perspective, planning and a concerted effort with real time policies we can explore all the vast economic options that lie before us waiting to be explored and obviously with huge benefits. As much of crude oil that we have we cannot compare with other oil producing nations of the world because most of them have diversified their economies therefore expanding the size of their economies and lifting their citizens beyond poverty. A phenomenon that still remains a huge dilemma in the Nigeria nation state.

It must be understood that population is not a curse giving the peculiarity of Nigeria in terms of its size as the most populous African Nation. Nigeria compared to most other African countries has been able to grow a little bit more, this is owing to the multiplicity of tribes, people with totally different cultures and ideologies cohabiting together as a nation. However not without its challenges as pointed out earlier. But the essence of this observation is to understand that the problem of economy is not one of huge population size, that it could be a huge blessing if proper and effective policies are brought to bear to the extent of engaging the entire population in a productive capacity, one which can really have a big positive impact on the economy. Nations like the United States of America and United Kingdom have achieved huge economic successes despite their huge population and even more diverse societies mixed with all peoples from every race thinkable in the world. Through focus, sincerity of purpose, and will power, they have put their nations on the platform of greatness and models for other nations to emulate in terms of their huge economic achievements. In a smaller capacity, Lagos state of Nigeria comparably in recent times has reciprocated such feats although in smaller capacities despite the huge challenges that confronts her. A result of purposefulness, willpower and focus at achieving development through resolution and in particular giving the multicultural nature of the state in terms of both its huge population and the diversity of ethnic, cultural and racial pluralism. In like manner it is just a very relevant inward and most suitable example to assert that indeed if the Nation wakes up to its responsibility nationally and do what is right with the economy, then Nigeria can progress economically just as much as other nation states of the world that have done so.

It is easy to fall into the trap of pointing accusing fingers at other nations as being responsible for our economic woes overtime, like the IMF or the London and Paris' clubs for plunging our nation into huge foreign loan debt through the interest rate placed on it. It is general knowledge that for a very long time Nigeria struggled annually to pay these huge loan debts which is irrational and economically disadvantageous as well as impoverishing our country for a long time until recent times when the government managed to pay off almost seventy percent of it. Generally Nigerians may blame the IMF and their cohort clubs for this gross injustice on Nigeria, firstly I would point out that the objective of the IMF and the world bank is to help poor and developing Nations of the world however they have given such loans to most poor countries of the world therefore further worsening their economic conditions. But the truth here is that objectively the fault is not theirs rather ours because we lack the ability to take the right decisions and strategies to drive growth and development and that is why these Nations have remained poor in the first place. We lack the drive and will power to proactively take the right decisions that will protect us from economic injustice and impoverishment caused us by lack of proper perspective and wisdom to act positively rather than naively and disadvantaged on the one hand while on the other hand the gross irresponsibility and lack of the drive of government to deliberately push growth and development. This is because our huge oil wealth and vast deposits of other natural economic resources is enough for us to thrive as a nation however our lack of knowledge of how to convert them into positive gains for the overall citizens of our country is the problem here. Our huge manpower if well tapped is such a great gift given our geographical vastness and richness as well as education and agriculture.

It is evident that most times we out source experts as majority of our professionals are incapable of really doing a proper and rest assuring job especially in the areas of engineering and practical science. All these is as a result of lack of initiative on the part of government to ensure an economically enabling environment whereby all these will be made possible to build local capacity and proficiency as well as a shift of a very bad ideological position of a craze for anything imported. I am not implying that we should not have economic relationship or trade with international agents but rather that our level of dependence is too much and grossly disadvantageous because it kills local capability and confidence. Another result of lack of value, trust and belief in ourselves and ability to do something positive. I will not talk much on the issues regarding education here because the next chapter discusses that. However I must point out that as regards economics much of our problems are still a result of a psycho mental distortion the result of lack of objectivity, confidence and believe in oneself or the ability to act proactively by oneself in a positive direction. Economics is not a rigid set of rules rather a virtual principle that is determined by human trade interactions and behaviors. Therefore economics pursuit like I once argued has an end goal in terms of all agents, that is, individuals, family, groups and society which is to take care of human welfare. As a law I went on to state further that the end of all economic endeavor or pursuit is welfare given that every human being engages in economic activities primarily because of the motive to earn a living so as to take care of personal welfare and it is this struggle for welfare in mind that makes agents strive economically in order to continuously meet the financial demand of welfare which can only be created by trade or legal services through the real and productive sector of the economy. Therefore we must also understand here that most of the real investment that can truly drive real growth are never financial investments but real investments in real estates, science and technology, education, agriculture, manpower and a whole lot of other real time investments. However backed by monetary finance. But the problem in Nigeria is that often than not we misrepresent investment for financial investment and downplaying real investments therefore fooling around with financial instruments without actual real sector backed resultant growth. This too is as a result of interest. It is fundamental to know that interest is not a real economic variable rather a false and artificial economic variable that was introduced by capitalism in order to serve their personal agenda of making others impoverished forever so as to serve them. Interest on money unfortunately has spread all over the world now and has become a very significant part of world economics. However the impact of interest is very damaging and often the cause of financial crises because when interest rates are fixed before the real sector investment outcome is determined then it is very immoral in the case of a loss because not only does the borrower has to pay the actual money borrowed but also an interest rate over it. This economic abnormality has become such a phenomenon that most economists fail to reason on it even when it is conventional economic knowledge that interest is a function of financial investment and not a function of real sector economics. But all the growth of economics only occurs in the real sector of the economy therefore if interests are charged all over the economy without real sector outcome it will eventually result into financial crises and the result is often the need for a bail out, it is the rationale behind the business cycle theory in economics. Because overtime the financial sector of the economies were built upon artificial variables thus the result of problems. However some economists often argue that the concern of economics is not normative but positive thus implying economics is not concerned about economic morality but rather positive dealings that is, what is but not what ought to be. The high time economics is refocused upon what ought to be would there be less crises like the world financial collapse because that is the result of error of judgment of founding fathers of economics who propounded the positive economics principle, unfortunately in contemporary times upon our claims of advancement beyond old times we illogically hold on to this dogma and repeat it over time as a standard for economic judgment. Rather than seeing through its weakness and defect, capitalist economists more so have used it as a basis of capitalist agenda and every one gouged their senses without common sense thus accepting it. Countries like Japan and China for their wise choices have left interest at zero percent for quite a while breaking out of western subjugation and oppression and the result is blossoming economies for both countries over the years and China especially at present is progressing at a very rapid rate beyond imagination. It is left to us too to see things clearly for ourselves and refuse to continue forever being slaves to others because whatever made them enslave us in the first place is not because we were created to be slaves of others but it is because we have allowed them do that to us by being narrow minded, naïve and unwise as to use our own senses to see what looks us in the face.

Another major cause of our problems is the lack of government to sincerely look into the wage structure of the nation. This particularly has a real impact on economic growth, development and stability.

I believe for the first time we can chart a leading course for Africa by forming a body of economic thinkers and strategists who would use their senses and form the Nigerian school of economic thought for the first time and influence our own economic destiny, the result which I believe if properly envisaged and engaged would result in positive effects and policies therefore charting a new beginning as well as a positive course for our nation economically also getting us out of the trap of intellectual slavery we have since been subjugated as a result of our lack of perspective and foresight.

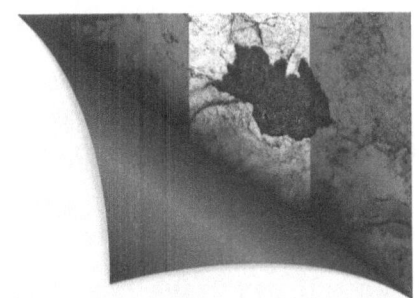

CHAPTER FOUR

EDUCATION

"THE ESSENCE OF EDUCATION IS NOT LEARNING BUT LIFE"

Education is the lifeblood through which any forward looking society flourishes, through direct impact and application in every aspect of human endeavor. Because the schools and other well funded educational institutions serve as the bridge between theory and practice, they are the bridge between knowledge and society thus supplying knowledge for societal benefit through well aimed researches, science and technological push and breakthrough, engineering progress and real time effective and applied knowledge to everyday societal advancement and progress. Developed nations the world over have paid tremendous attention to their educational sector more so to the extent that it remains among their topmost budget priorities. Forward looking nations till date have never underestimated the importance of education in and on the society. the constant attainment of advancement in terms of human existence whether in science, technology, Arts, sports, Engineering, Economics and all areas of human life endeavor has overtime been attained through constant research, and by research I mean effective research. By the earliest sentence of this chapter is meant, whatever education is, it's main objective is so that it can benefit human lives vis avis our real time day to day activities and existence as well as making life easy for all of us in general as humanity. whereby the primary objective of this is the attainment of knowledge through which we can then apply it in practice. However when the objective of education is misplaced, it becomes very worthless because even then it fails to achieve what it was meant for. Worse still educational essence when misunderstood often times lead to further societal problems because those who seemingly are perceived educated are not but rather academic slaves having not understood still the essence of education thus seeing education from a remote perspective therefore limiting the extent to which education can be beneficial, and in this situation worse more when most of such people affected are university professors, academics or school teachers. The attendant effect being a disoriented society one stagnant in terms of educational progress even though seemingly educationally active but least efficient at achieving the essence of education.

Educational impact has never been insignificant, the least of which is space exploration. Man overtime has made important discoveries influenced by educational advancement the world over, whether it is in the areas of computer science and technology, health care, automobiles, ship crafts, fast trains and housing to mention a few. All these have been the achievement of countries that understand the importance of such actions, thus investing hugely in them.

A people without educational push are a lost people, lost in the sense that they have lost the purpose for their existence, the need to discover at every point in time the essence of existence itself. Through human interactions, as well as a sound knowledge of our environment and above all our communication with our creator Almighty God through the metaphysical cognition of ourselves, mental, physical and transcendental as well.

Much of our national educational structure and policies are not much beneficial in terms of real impact on the general well being of our socio-economic development as a people. Why we still rely so much on external help when we have to do anything practical, the least is to use the example of sports where we hardly believe in our local coaches to tutor our teams in the most internationally professional standard to say the least. It doesn't mean we cannot employ foreign trainers, however what I mean is that we lack the proactive nature that puts in place structures and programs where local talents can be developed to international competitive standards where such people can be useful not just locally but also widely sought internationally as well. It is no news that over the years when Nigeria has had to attend an international sports competition especially football tournaments, we often at the last stages preceding the competitions sack local coaches who worked hard to qualify the team for such tournaments employing foreign coaches where by the salaries dished out to them are almost one hundred percent more than what was paid our local coaches. Perhaps they our local team coaches lack the wherewithal no matter where they got their training from. This is one of the many pathetic cases of the Nigerian society, a proof of lack of self confidence or the drive and ability to use our common sense, to improvise, to sit down and look deep into things, try many things, the ability to learn and make mistakes in order to really know something. One interesting and very important observation is that I have realized that the African mentality is structured against mistakes, although there are some mistakes that are costly and disliked but what I mean here is the mistakes made when learning something new. There just has to be trials and errors in order to arrive at certainty. However, we are too impatient and unwilling to make such mistakes, we always want everything fast and ready, where as it is against the real wisdom of knowledge. The fear of mistakes in learning is an easy path to mediocrity as most times the underlying facts elude us as regards the basis of that knowledge. For example, Thomas Edison when trying to discover the incandescent light, was said to have made over a hundred mistakes before eventually getting it right. The result of his never give up spirit is the result of the electric bulbs or lamps we use all over the world now. More intriguing about Edison's attitude is his conviction and confidence that as matter of fact when asked why he had failed several times before finally getting it right his reply was positive, he responded convinced that he however did not fail those number of times rather that he discovered the many ways by which an incandescent lamp cannot be made. What a positive belief he had. Therefore this example shows us that as a people we must be willing to take actions and be proactive towards our existence by realizing that we can actually do things too ourselves if we actually take time to collectively develop a spirit of positivity and an attitude of tolerance, love and respect for one another as well as positive encouragements always. This is very fundamental to a peaceful coexistence as against division, lack of love and disrespect or intolerance has been the order of our societies.

The educational sciences and technology in perspective are key to modern day strength and stability of nations the world over. Most leading nations today like the U.S.A, Great Britain, Russia, Japan, Germany, China and the rest are very much ahead in terms of science and technological push giving them the edge and an advantage in world affairs. These nations are strong and constantly improving what they have and further discovering new inventions. As the world becomes more advanced, it is very important that wise nations follow suit in understanding the nature of these trends as well as making concerted efforts to be knowledgeable in this issues in order to be able to cope in a changing world. Many other reasons abound as well why nations must be alert and prepared to take up researches into areas of science and technology in order to protect themselves especially in a world where you never can fully trust people with your lives. Just like the case of European occupation of Africa a long time ago. They were only able to because they had the sophistication and superiority of knowledge and wisdom with which they planned and strategized in every areas of their operations in order to take what they want. The historical events of these occupation was brutal and wicked as a lot of wrong and injustice was done on our people. But we have forgiven them, however the problem is that we haven't learned at all. While the scope of operation is different in this modern age, they perhaps are doing even worse to us still. Yet the result of our own faults, a psycho mental distortion that constantly holds us in an illusion of a bitter oblivion of our reality. Our scientists hardly can produce anything practical beyond the theoretical knowledge that limits them. The framework of knowledge that they process is often less applied in a real world situation because they hardly can keep up with practice perhaps the foundation of their knowledge is not strong enough to be productive in real terms. There is no pretty much significant invention that we can point at or mention which has been made locally. The problem is not the lack of the capability of our local engineers to invent but the lack of a proper educational framework to support them in order to achieve similar feats as is done in most advanced countries of the world.

The academic structure is long overdue for an overhaul, the stagnant and unprogressive attitude of our policy makers can very much be seen here again, the lack of a will power, the languidity of a people towards purpose, a lack of the proper perspective through which things are done in their most proper manner. Unnecessary bureaucratic hindrances as well have since contributed to educational stagnancy and lack of proper education of the policy makers themselves in whose hands lie the responsibility to effect positive and forward looking measures for education in the Nation called Nigeria. And this remains the same problem over and over time. The same mistakes, naivety and lack of perspective by the administrations to effect a proper framework in order to propel the educational content of the country at large so as to create a meaningful impact on the socio-economic and political condition at large.

"knowledge is power" they say, but knowledge without know how is meaningless. Worse still, when someone is believed to possess some particular knowledge but lack the proper perspective of that knowledge or doesn't know how to put it into use then such knowledge is at that point not beneficial because such a person perhaps might not even be able to identify the proper place of such knowledge. It is therefore important that knowledge is aimed at getting the seeker of it out of naivety, this is very important, at least in that specific area of knowledge that such a person may possess. It is very bad when one claims to have a particular knowledge and then still remain naïve in that area of knowledge. This is the case often times in the Nigerian scenario where by most of the education rendered doesn't in most cases prepare one for the reality of its practicality. They are often times theory oriented and overemphasized beyond their application.

The impact of government on academics is very important because it is government that is responsible for the educational policies that is effected by the academic institutions, therefore government must work hand in hand with real time academics at ensuring that proper educational policies are enacted, ones which are forward looking as well as allocating proper funds to meet the productive demand of educational activities. Looking around us we would realize that libraries are almost nonexistent. In most developed countries you find a library in every county however in our own community it is not so. Even the few libraries that exist are falling apart and lack adequate funding and management. It is therefore important that we also take into cognizance this defect in our ideology. It is because we don't value such things that is why we don't invest in them.

Also the attitude of our academics must be changed as regards their approach to education, constant intimidation of students and an overlord behavior by lectures where by students fear lecturers too much is not a healthy situation to nurture educational productivity. While respect and courtesy is required by students towards their teachers it does not mean that teachers cannot have a close and healthy communication with their students in as much as there is trust and respect between them. The scenario is often times one of bullying, intimidation, discouragement and a too strict approach by teachers especially at the high school level. It is very wrong and unproductive because it hardens the minds of these students in a wrong way and even give some of them wrong belief that they cannot succeed.

Our responsibility as a nation is to do everything possible to educate every citizen of the nation in the best way because the resultant effect is often development and stability like recent cases of countries like Singapore who on the journey to development achieved seventy five percent educated population of the overall population of their country. Now Singapore is counted amongst the advanced nations of the world.

It is therefore up to us to take up a challenge against our overtime suppressive mindset and start a change towards development.

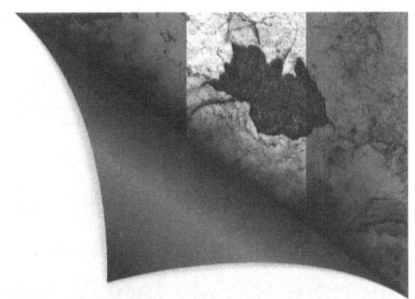

CHAPTER FIVE

HUMANITY AND THE RULE OF LAW

Humanity is indeed a great issue and particularly in a more diverse world order. The existence of peoples of different racial backgrounds, ethnicity, tribe and family across the world makes the issue of humanity more complex. However the vastness and spread of human beings all over, one thing is true and certain. The fact that humanity is one. We often all agree that we all came from Adam and Eve, multiplying into nations, races, tribes, ethnicities and various divisions you can ever think of. Our overtime fractionalization as one Humanity lead us to forget the lineage we all share which is Adam and Eve. We often characterize ourselves as superior or better depending on where we fall. This is not to say that all peoples must be equal at once, but for the purpose of humanity for what it truly means, we must understand the reality of the oneness that gave birth to humanity and the reason why it so is. The world today is full of chaos, injustice, oppression, cruelty, intolerance, wars and so on. The result of inhumanity and lack of proper understanding of our commonness in diversity. There are no lesser humans as far as I believe, although the human society today is guilty of this error of classification. Many a times is the society responsible for injustice because of lack of sincere humanity. Though you hear often times all around, calls for humanity services, however misunderstood and built on misconceptions in a larger perspective. I am not saying that there aren't those who sincerely strive on the course of humanity rather that the core society that is responsible for humanity has erred in its duty for what it truly means. Humanity simply put as I understand it is the peaceful coexistence of humans in a just society. A society where by human beings are fairly and equally treated without sacred cows or exceptions to the rule. A society where by all people collectively strive against injustice without fear of favor. A society where by everyone looks after everyone in order to maintain true peace in the entire society. A society where people have rest of mind.

The Nigerian nation today is a typical example of a nation where you find peoples of different languages and cultures. It therefore is a very good case study of humanity. The situation of Nigeria is complex as we have said earlier giving the diversity in ideological differences that surrounds her, but the extent of diversity is not the problem in a multifaceted society but the lack of a true humanistic principle for all outcomes. In a country where humanistic values are lost all else is lost because the standard of human unity is justice, equity and fairness. To peacefully cohabit under a just law in order to keep things in orderliness. The rule of law is thus a collective binding upon the society as a whole where by the law becomes the standard of judgment upon every member of the community. The law should not and must not be built on wrong principles or unrealistic ideologies, but a common reasoning on the general values of the society in which it subsists. However where faulty laws exists it becomes the duty of the society to rectify such laws in order to do justice to what humanity stands for. The Nigerian society has a lot of shortcomings as regards human rights and fair justice. The inhuman way by which the ordinary man is maltreated by uniformed men is a very good case of the gross injustice of our society. Members of the society should be treated with care and respect for humanity sake. There are many cases too where some people in high positions have maltreated there odlies because of the power they posses. All these thrive because of the weakness of law and justice in the society. The autocratic Boss syndrome.

Looking at the major cause of this problem going from our antecedent we would realize that it still has to do with the problem of a psycho mental distortion whereby we wield too much power and behave with tyranny. The society is structured in a way that every boss is an overlord. Imagine the many cases of house owners slapping their gatemen or car owners slapping their drivers just because they are in their employ. It is very disheartening that all these persist, the worst thing is that we never take into consideration these little things not to talk of correcting it. We have seen societies that are very advanced and developed, there people freely communicate with their leaders and some even express open discontent with their leaders and yes it remains their opinion and they have a right to it. It is called freedom of speech. However many a times have people been arrested for saying what is in their mind as a result of anger and frustration at injustice, even where laws seemingly exist to protect that, government authorities have in the past turned deaf ears to the cry for justice and even arrantly disobey the rule of law. It Is high time we reorganized this crazy structure so as to propel our nation forward positively.

A lot of commendations must sincerely go to the judiciary whom overtime has displayed courage in the face of intimidation and oppression against injustice by giving fair judgment in many cases especially cases of election petition tribunal. It is very well commended and encouraged because the judiciary stands as the final rule of law and must realize that they have a right to be protected and maintained because the job of the judiciary like I have always thought is very important and sensitive. The judiciary must be independent and free of external influence because it is the property of the entire nation. Whatever funds comes to it from the executive is its due right and whatever security is given to it is its due right as well because they have a very sensitive job and while every member of the society cannot be a judge it is very fundamental that they be well maintained in order to do justice to the rule of law that they swear to protect, uphold and preserve. Every member of the society too is important but we must all realize that we all need a trustworthy justice system in order to be assured of true justice without favor or bias at every point in time.

A just society is the dream of every reasonable human being because such condition would give such a person rest of mind and assurance that they are safe from oppression and where it occurs they can very well get a fair rule of law. It is thus our collective duty and responsibility to ensure that true justice is upheld, protected and preserved for the sake of peace and humanity.

CHAPTER SIX

ORGANIZATION

The term Organization by itself could mean different things, for example a business organization, a political organization or a student's organization, however in this chapter the term organization was carefully conceived in its most basic meaning which can be explained as the art of careful planning and execution of an action of interest or urgency or anything that generally needs to be done. Most times when someone is responsible for committing an error of action we are quick to conclude that such persons are not well organized. But in real perspective organization is not lack of trying at all rather it is the real ability to systematically arrange the order of needs with careful observation of every detailed requirement and employing every material needed at every stage of the process to achieve a most desirable result. Organization thus is a perfect preparation in advance for every decision or step taken in a well studied manner to achieve success. Organization is thus a very important part of human life without proper and adequate organization we cannot function effectively and worse more without the required knowledge of proper organization we cannot succeed.

It is with this background that we observe the national organizational structure in its reality.

The question is judging from the earlier paragraph, Is the Nigerian organizational structure as a nation well conceived, planned and achieved? Obviously the answer is no. This is certainly because we have a defective organizational structure or. Organization like we said can only be effective when well targeted at its fundamental need. Like the case of a family organization for example, the father and mother are the directors of the organization, though the father is often the chief director and grand commander of the order of the family. Their primary needs are food, shelter and clothing. According to proper organization the parents are the organizers and their management of the family depends on the level of their organizational skills because now they are faced with external factors in the management of their nuclear family. External factors like societal competition, finance, education and civil law among others. Since individuals cannot completely exist in isolation and away from society it then becomes a matter of organizational skills and know how as well as perfection to survive against unfavorable influences such as bad societal influence on the children as well as other numerous examples however, giving guiding factors such as religiosity and morality as well as the rule of law to serve as a deterrence to wrong actions. So in most cases where there is a short fall of responsibility on the parts of the parents it has an effect on the children. This is because there are some fundamental needs that must be provided and can only be provided by the parents for the children like the Government, there are very basic structures and needs that must be adequately provided for the generality of every member of the society within the national wealth as a priority and most essential requirement of any effective national organization. If the government fails in this it then becomes an error of knowledge, skills or know how and in such cases such government are irresponsible and unfit govern because they lack the most basic understanding of proper and effective National organization and where such exist there cannot be any positive achievement because the foundation upon which everything else is built is missing and until the foundation of the organizational structure is built there will never be a concrete progress. In the case of National Organization it even becomes more complex because unlike the nuclear family where maybe the shortfall of a parent can be compensated for by another parent or other members of the extended family directly it becomes impossible because of the Nation status, most times external charities don't do justice to the crisis of poverty and incomes disparity across boards, it is still solely the responsibility of government to provide basic amenities and the platform for which wealth can spread and poverty eliminated through proper organization, planning and execution across all quarters of the society.

The underlying problem is still one of lack of the proper perspective to prioritize and understand the dynamics of proper organizational structuring for effectively meeting the needs and demands of the society as a nation. The fault of the Nigerian government overtime has been an unnecessary fist clenching on tasks and responsibilities that are better executed by the state or local government or even the private sectors. Instead of allocating tasks to their proper jurisdictions for a very long time the federal government has involved itself with too much than it can handle therefore resulting in inhuman consequences all over the nation. A typical example is the Electric Authority of

Nigeria where government has failed consistently and it still clench its fists on it without letting go to state governments or private organizations who can better handle the job. But unfortunately where government has let go of such industries, like the telecoms, it has done a very bad job at regulation, most of the telecoms companies are a rip off to the masses, the charges are grossly too expensive compared to other countries where they operate and who is to blame for such ill treatments, obviously the government who allowed them. It is unfair how our own government can sell us out consistently against the plight of the generality of our people. One of the major undoing of the nation is the mismanagement of the petroleum sector, where since inception there has consistently been a sabotage of the few existing refineries, government instead of ensuring refineries are built and operating to full capacity of national daily petroleum demand have actually turned deaf hears to that need, rather deciding to subsidize petroleum. Interestingly recently the present day government cried foul of the injustice of fuel subsidy, they claim it has no effect on the masses because importers of fuel are feeding fat and claiming subsidy revenues without actually supplying their claimed imported fuel to local consumption. Most of the subsidy claims have been bogus and inimical to the effective channeling of our yearly financial budget to developmental needs. However the statistics shows the sorry state of a lack of respect for the constitution of the masses who form the nation State, the gross and arrant disregard for the basic right of the people not to mention their full right. In broad day light our government have fooled us and constantly maligned us, they have cheated and stolen everything away from us and at the same time bullied us without recourse to change. There is no question of transparency. It is another sorry and naïve situation where by people demand for transparency, what more needs to be transparent? That the government is irresponsible enough to harbor importation of crude oil into our country when we have consistently earned enough crude oil wealth to transform our nation beyond imagination into a beautiful and desired nation of sort. Nigeria could have been like Japan, U.S.A or Europe at least in terms of their developmental achievement. That is the result of naivety and illiteracy when people can't even see the true picture. That government has been unaccountable for the oil wealth over these years is enough evidence against it. What about the billions of national revenue allocated to the power sector development that was stolen by the government officers in charge of it and aided by the foreign contractors. What else has been done till date about it to make sure that the money is retrieved and the offenders prosecuted. That we import refined oil in a country that has abundant crude oil is a shame and a big economic error. The effect is that government over the years has thrown away a huge income multiplier through value added by the refineries, also the vast opportunities that abound as a result of the refineries' service sectors is a big loss. Is it to say that the government doesn't know all of these all these years? A psycho mental Distortion a naïve sell off of oneself over to a wiser onlooker. This is the case of the Nigeria Condition. While the nations of the world have labeled us with all sorts of bad names, indeed our youths too have gotten involved in all sorts of financial crimes to say the least. Worse more crimes that are unheard have been committed by those in the government and their abettors and get away without indictment and in few cases of indictment they are given light punishment. Well another error of the justice system, the consequence of executive interference in our justice system. Everyone seems to have lost hope. The manner by which Nigerians are often treated abroad is very unfortunate and sad. Every Nigerian is a suspect and interestingly even our government officials including diplomats. Well shall we say serves us right. That is what we did to ourselves. Whereas our problem is not one that has no cure rather a staunch recourse to indifference, languidity against a positive change a reluctance and worse more a resistance to change the status quo.

I believe we can put behind our bitter past and reorganize our national organizational structure, re write our history and change our condition to a beautifully positive one if we all cure ourselves of the disease of a perverse mindset the consequence of a psycho mental distortion we can all change our old and negative ways of live. Just as I was going to write this sentence I heard the azaan(the Islamic call to prayer)and I looked outside the window of my apartment in Amman. As I tried tracing the location of the big and beautiful blue Masjid (Prayer house)in respect and observance of the azaan with its sweet rhythm, I happened on a team of road constructing engineers and workers fixing a small portion of the road leading adjacent to the main road that divides my part of the county and the other side. The imagination is left to the reader especially the Nigerian who is well conversant to the problems of road dilapidation in the country. How responsive is our government or road caretakers to such responsibilities as is due. Perhaps the lack of proper organization and management and a lack of the sense of urgency and task as it demands.

The problem of organization is caused by a lack of will power or resolution to be organized as a people to take charge and responsibility, effectively and urgently as is required every time so as to meet urgent requirements and needs constantly. Until we do things properly and allocate checks and balances with effective and resultant action plans constantly only will we achieve organizational efficiency.

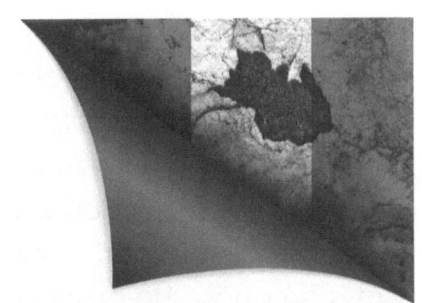

CHAPTER SEVEN

DREAMS

This chapter hopes to express our collective hopes and desires for Nigeria in terms of what we hope to see happen in our blessed country Nigeria soon. They are not different from most of the general wishes and dreams of every Nigerians out there both home and abroad.

Collectively our driving force being the good of our fellow humans. The joy of seeing everyone happy and fulfilled. We should despise oppression, injustice and wickedness in all forms.

It is very important to realize that collective interest is very important for general stability, like shared National interest and happines. It doesn't mean we don't have private moments of happiness, like when one suddenly happens on a deep realization of the oneness of God and his supremacy. Or when we suddenly realize the essence of life (God: through humanity, love, unity and peace) to get to God you must go through humanity. because every saint that ever lived passes through humanity.

I dream of a Nigeria soon that is totally at peace across all facets of the society. A Nigeria that is among the leading nations in clean science and technological development for the benefit of humanity and not the crazy desire for weapons of mass destruction.

I dream of a Nigeria that has top and leading universities amongst leading universities all over the world. To see in the nearest future a situation where Nigerians are flocking back home because Nigeria achieves a socio economic status that is amongst the best in the world.

I wish for a Nigeria where there is true justice and equity, peace and love across all ideological divides.

A future whereby Nigerians are Proud once more to be Nigerians where ever they are as well as maintaining the good Image that we must have attained.

I wish for a Nigeria where there is equal opportunity as well as abundance for livelihood. A beautiful and well organized Nigeria whereby government is proactive to the needs of the people.

A Nigeria where there is sincere motive by people to take up government offices because they truly want to serve and are really qualified and capable to.

A Nigeria where we appreciate ourselves and one another as well as placing high importance on local capacity development and know how across all facets of the society.

A Nigeria that has truly arrived and no more judged by the mistake of our past leaders but a New Nigeria well respected and loved across the world.

EPILOGUE

"All actions are judged according to their intentions and everyone is rewarded according to what he intends".

Prophet Muhammad (peace and blessings be upon Him)

Hopefully what is intended with this book is self realization and awakening for humanity. An awakening that breeds love, peace and unity.

As people we can be progressive, proactive, leading and respectable amongst other nations of the world. With optimism and conviction of the possibility of a resultant mind change-conditional change effect, I foresee a Nigeria and Africa that is ready to change, to say to the world with a beautiful smile: it is a new begining, We take responsibility for our attitudes, our conditions and our lives. We shall no more be naïve! We are a changed people, ready to properly manage our own resources. We shall respect every single member of our people, protect them and support them home and abroad. The same positive attitude nurtured by progressive nations. We shall henceforth love one another and gloriously shall we flourish together.

The true birth of a true great nation, greatness that has long been overshadowed by our lack of perspective, a failing realization of our potential and collective abilities our song now shall be thank you God for the blessing of humanity and had we realized earlier we would have long been at peace. We would have realized the power of unity in diversity for what it truly means. We would have taken real and effective advantage of it for the benefit of one another. The simple secret, being that, everyone must look out for the other. It is called sincere rallying round.

We must stop all division and apartheid. A division that has long been a major contribution to our former milieu. It is time to rise together collectively, and all bitterness, anger, frustration and hatred sincerely put to end and forgotten. All accusing hands seize and a sincerely new chapter begun. A new antecedent written and standardized as well as clearly written with uniqueness to our needs and ideologies. Since all ideologies mustn't be in contrary to the true spirit of humanity, no selfish agenda must be entertained, for a sincere, just, correct and well represented consensus cannot produce a faulty judgment. All selfish and hidden agenda must be dropped by all for the benefit of all and sundry. For a true nation flourishes by justice and equity.